# EXILE ON A GRID ROAD

# EXILE ON A GRID ROAD

SHELLEY BANKS

*thistledown press*

Thistledown Press Ltd.
410 2nd Ave. North
Saskatoon, Saskatchewan, S7K 2C3
www.thistledownpress.com

Library and Archives Canada Cataloguing in Publication
Banks, Shelley, 1955–, author
Exile on a grid road / Shelley Banks.
Poems.
ISBN 978-1-77187-057-3 (paperback)
I. Title.
PS8603.A6243E95 2015     C811'.6     C2015-905171-1

Cover design by Stephanie Strain
Book design by Jackie Forrie
Cover photograph by Shelley Banks
Author photograph by Gord Hunter
Printed and bound in Canada

Canada Council    Conseil des Arts
for the Arts      du Canada

SASKATCHEWAN
ARTS BOARD

Canada

Thistledown Press gratefully acknowledges the financial support of the Canada Council for the Arts, the Saskatchewan Arts Board, and the Government of Canada for its publishing program.

# Acknowledgements

With thanks to all who encouraged the development of this book, including the network of writers I've met in Regina and at retreats, and the writers I worked with in the University of B.C.'s MFA Creative Writing program, especially Susan Musgrave and my poetry classmates, as well as Peter Levitt, all of whom provided insights on an early draft of parts of this manuscript.

Several of these poems have been published in literary magazines, including *Carousel*, *Room*, *Other Voices*, *The Society* and *Spring*, and were included in submissions that placed as finalists in the City of Regina Writing Award and in the Saskatchewan Writers' Guild's Short Manuscript Awards.

I'd also like to recognize the Saskatchewan Arts Board for its support, the Saskatchewan Artists/Writers Retreats Program for providing space at St. Peter's Abbey to write, and the Sage Hill Writing Experience for igniting my interest in poetry. I am grateful to the people at Thistledown, in particular Al Forrie and Jackie Forrie for production, publishing and all the rest, and to Michael Kenyon for his support and editorial guidance. I'd also like to thank the Bees for writing friendships, and Friday Night Floor Hockey for writing talk (and beer).

Finally, my love and thanks to my family, for recognizing my absent-mindedness and making sure that I remember to eat, sleep and enjoy life.

# CONTENTS

*For Gord,*
*Morgan and Chris*


*If you read this . . .*

# High Wire

The psychic takes my palm,
looks blankly past me, says
You were a boy in the Depression.

How are you with heights?
I don't tell her that I never
let my kids climb jungle gyms,
never pushed them arcing to the sky
on metal swings. I am afraid
of soaring too high,
the fall.

Have you ever seen a circus?
I don't tell her of the one
I saw at twenty-two.
Migraine pounding, nauseated
by the smell of sawdust, I ran
outside the tent and sat alone.

Do you like gymnastics?
I don't tell her I can't
put my trust in gravity unless
my feet are on the ground.

I see you on the high wire.
So young,
so light.

I tell myself I don't believe, and yet I mourn
this new-found shadow self along my lifeline,
the orphan acrobat who leapt
from his trapeze and lost
my spirit, eighty years ago.

# I Can't Hold to the Present

The mountain ash by the back fence drops
leaves, its berry clusters shrivel. Poisoned,
you say. Blame the neighbour, the man

who walks the alley every evening
in a pin-striped suit, spraying
Round-Up on daisies, black-eyed

Susans, dandelions. High on a poplar, one leaf
lurches out and spins, then settles where it hangs.
Beyond, the sky is pewter blue, the clouds slate

submarines patrolling the horizon. Crabapples
cling to branches by the door, bite-sized
red marbles, bitter on grey bark. No robins,

grackles, gulls. Winter comes. Frost glitters
on the windows of my van. I scratch your name
across the windshield with my key, turn up

the heater, melt the ice. When quackgrass,
burdock grow again in spring, you'll chop
that tree for firewood. Ash to ashes. Strike a match.

# Snow Geese

In the marsh south of the airport
snow geese rise. Then, necks thrust
forward, wing tips curled,
they drop down to November

grass. You lied. You never loved me.
If I had my way, I'd make you
clean this marsh, pick up every
feather with your teeth.

It's cold here and the air is salty,
thick with rain before a storm.

I want to fly
above the disappearing
islands to my home.

# On the Harvest Moon

the CN freight is silent
when we come down
from the shrine

where Mary stands
with lightning rods
in white carrara marble

blessing pilgrims
with Grand Marnier
and songs.

Driving home, the radio
crackles, the window mists
with grid road dust,
and as we rise up
from a hollow, we see

brake lights, a car
stopped
mid-road, in

darkness

praying to the shadow
boxcars rocking
down the line

the night so
wide we think we are

the last.

# Agribition

I walk past iron signs of horses,
wolves and cowboys, past
the Watkins man who will deliver
dill and pure vanilla to my farm, past
rows of hand-tooled leather boots

into the barn. My city's skin
lifts here, its urban face
a mask over this flesh
of hay and horses, hammering hoofs.

Eyes wild, Suri kicks the metal gate.
until the women come and stroke her nose, her neck.
She nuzzles fingers.
"She is so homesick," say the women,
with their riding boots and horse sense.

I back away from cinnamon-soft
Belgians, Percherons who prance,
manes braided, hoofs painted shiny black.

I have no farm.
I am three generations past my mother's flight
from saddles, curry combs and dill.

I am afraid of horses.
I'm city-deep, no secret
country core, no cowboy
boots or raffle tickets on the chestnut mare.

"She is so lonely," say the women,
with their riding boots and horse sense.

And demolition thunders
from the filly's stall up to the roof.

# Exile on a Grid Road

I want to know their names,
the natives and exotics,
everything that flourishes,
sun-baked, neglected,
on this gravel road.

Would I belong if I could tell
milk vetches from alfalfa?
Could I stay longer
with every plant named?
A week for yarrow, two
for goat's beard, three
for groundsel, more.

Beside me, dragonflies
flash on wild chamomile.

# Late Rains

Deer paw at stalks
of red fife wheat
deep under drifts
in Pete's field,
the one he didn't harvest
before the weather changed.

He cut and stooked
but the rains came,
then the snow.

Last evening, six deer.
Now thirty.

Coyotes circle.

# Carcass Walk

Sinews poke
from frozen ankles,
scraps of hide
grow frost fur.

Last night's
yips and howls
rumour a wolf
has joined the hunt.

Today, fresh kills startle
the field, blood-
laced, devoured
to the breastbone.

# Undone

Two weeks of rain.
The backyard sinks
from grass to mud to slurry,
and dogs stamp
small dead animals
across our floors.

The rain unleashes
blossoms from crabapples,
strolls from evenings,
passion from compassion,
all restraints undone.

Today, I wake at five
and once more watch
the windows stream with rain.

I miss reggae and calypso.
I've forgotten
how to dance.
I can no longer speak
the languages.

But most, I miss
the dry land,
pink petals
before rain.

# Prairie Icon

Your eyes glitter dark
suspicion. I have peanuts
and warm hands
for your scaly feet
but there's no trust
when claws grip fingers.
Only hunger. Cold. Need

betrays. You exchange
fear for nuts and I discard
respect in quest of a photograph.
Each feather flashes

knife-sharp, wings, tail
pleated black, white, pearl,
smoke.

# Raw Desire

Late winter. Morning.
I follow drifts and deer tracks,
stumble, lurch, and then

wide wings streaked brown
swoop low over barbed wire
into the windbreak trees.

A Great Horned Owl.
Its flight too swift to capture.
'Capture.'

One breath, but one breath only
before greed — the need not to believe
but prove this presence — rushes in

and the memory of the great
owl's soaring grace
flounders in desire,

reduced
to just another checklist photo
lost.

# Listening to Thunder

Under lichen, rocks. Wait.
The stillness
of rain.

# They Say I've Settled in. Well . . .

when I started
i was thirty-nine feet tall

higher than lamp posts
longer than the wind

but stress
made me

small

after three weeks
i no longer had to bow
through doorways

at five months
i couldn't reach the light switch
at eight, i'd lost the desk

but i guess i've settled in well
now that i'm crawling with the rest

# The Strike Drags On

### Day 7

Pick up the phone.
Tape interviews.
Listen to the news.

On my desk, a media log curls:
*Reporters say you said the same thing yesterday,*
*so cut the bullshit, fax us secret files,*
*and are committees and comités the same,*
*and do they have separate heads?*
Then sums up, oh-so-politely rightly:
*No comment today for broadcast news.*

### Day 16

Go to meetings.
Check the Net.
Draft thank-you notes
for other staff.

My braid has come undone.
My tea is cold and tastes like chewing gum.
Someone retypes my notes
without my blessing or my Word doc.
No one answers e-mails. The message
light is blinking. Ten new calls.

### Day 28

Interrupt discussions.
Write down names
and times and numbers.

The sun glares through
my bird-stained window
and the peace lilies
that never bloom
wilt on the carpet.

Outside, two pigeons
peck and bicker,
strut and shit
across ice floes on the tar
and gravel roof below.

### Day 34

Tape. Type. Talk.

I have an obit as a screen saver
this morning, a photo from the funeral
that I missed yesterday.

I'm so tired I could fall asleep
in the Lysol wipes I hope
will keep me safe from colds and flu,
will keep me healthy . . . working . . . here . . .

### Day 39

Check e-mails.
Check my voice mail.
Sweat in winter sunshine.

### Day 40

Start again.

# How to Improve Employee Satisfaction

Who donated the CIA's *Nicaragua Manual*
to this office book sale? *Planned Failures
of Capitalism* for the United Way?

What *Radical Priest*
works here, goes home
to Thomas Merton, Marx,
and *The Essential Lenin?*

I watch my colleagues enter,
leave, then quietly return.

How carefully
they hide themselves
beneath black jackets
and Italian leather shoes.

No one buys *Hiking and Backpacking,
Low Fat Cooking,* or *Zapp! How to Improve
Quality, Productivity and Employee Satisfaction.*

But *Guerilla Warfare*
is gone.

# You'll Call in Sick Today

because your heart rate accelerates
like hard rock convertibles
because your office has fevers
too vicious to fight
because your puppy's tail gets cropped
by the stupid trap door
because you drink too much
Glenfiddich, then dry red wine

because the plague rats say ignore them
chest rattles go away
because palpitations make you almost
plough into a fire truck
because every time she wags now
she shows you her severed tip
because it's better to be pissed off
than pissed on

because you yearn to float in sunlight
not struggle in fluorescent
because it's fiscal year-end
and you've found out who'll be fired
because the fever train is on your track
razors in your sinus and throat
because poppy seeds of blood mist
your seat, book, table, page

# The Day after Layoffs

I trudge back to the office,
my boots scuffing tire-packed snow.

Then, pinned in ice, a bird
  dead
      but so beautiful.

One feathered wing
          outstretched.

Pterodactyl in sandstone.

# The Excuses She Makes

I'm on time and busy, bitter
that she's late
again.

Lost, drunk, travelling,
a new boyfriend,
shopping, asleep.

I have heard it all and I am tired
of covering her lack of work,
her absences.

And yet, I want the joy she finds
in shunning the daily nine to five.

This girl who slides in late
after two-hour lunches, wears Black Cashmere,
come-fuck-me shoes.

Who never regrets
the excuses she makes
for living.

# Midnight

Someone's head is on your pillow,
forearm heavy on your chest,
and you're lying in the damp
spot on the sheets.

Attraction or adventure?
Were you curious
or drunk? Flattered
or in love? Offered
jewelry, drugs, a job?

They're outside your room
now with their clipboards
and checkboxes, counting
two-hundred-and-thirty-seven
reasons why

humans have sex.

Were you trying
to hurt a rival?
Relieve menstrual cramps?

Celebrate a birthday, change
the conversation,
say goodbye?

Why not say
you pray
to Aphrodite,
her seam foam,
pomegranates, pearls?

Or better still,
don't talk.

Lock that door.

# Swordfish

The rules are deliciously
simple.

A naked single has only one
valid candidate.

That does not mean all
naked singles are simple
to spot.

Identifying naked pairs
does not necessarily mean
immediate conversion.

The top and bottom regions
hold the clues.

Beyond pairs, we also encounter
naked, hidden triplets, quads, even quints.

The pleasure comes
from the different types.
The principle is exactly the same.

Swordfish. Skyscraper. Squirmbag. X-wing.

It's all down to spotting the clues.

# It's all about Pi

if you loved me you'd explain
    *three  point  one  four  one  five  nine*

        that's why
        I'm hiding
        in the cellar

you'd explain so I would understand
    *two  six  five  three  five*

        upstairs
        his girlfriend cries
        over science she's assigned

I'd understand pi, if you only loved me
    *eight  nine  seven  nine*

        this circle can't be squared
        I can't divide
        misalliance

if you explained, I'd understand
    *three  two  three  eight  four  six  two*

        I'd try
        but I can't exorcise
        transcendence

it's all about pi . . . and do you love me?
    *six  four  three  three  eight*

        add a trillion more

        irrational constants
        never stop

# Too Dry to Wash Betrayal from our Skin

Somewhere, students rise after a shooting, a genocide trial
seethes and fans fight over Lennon's towel. Let it be. We're on
the grid road now, and static cackles that there's no good way
to say goodbye. Each sparrow dawn, old memories bubble. The
grass and leaves sway whiskey gold and broken bottles gleam like
diamonds.

At my old job, we only talked of strategies and rain. Now, you
take stock of potholes, while I analyze my mother's melt-water
decline. She doesn't know her own phone number, sees nothing
but her shadow cast above dark mountains in a rainbow ring. It
takes more miles than this to hear the ghost down in the valley,
the echo of the bluebird's bones.

In the classifieds, I find an ad for part-time evening cleaners. Can
they sparkle dusks after all mornings have smeared incessant dirt
onto our afternoons, and dank residues of spin have sifted down
to tilt our dreams? Garbage wears a brand name, and one blue-
black iridescent feather. Dust clouds far below chart truck routes
on the valley floor. Eagles soar.

A woman hunches at the crossroads, crying. She's lost her ring,
yellow gold with diamonds. Identities can fracture in an instant.
You are not the boy I knew; I never was the woman you desired.
Sing a song of Yesterday's Camel, once so fit to survive Beringia's
cold. Bumblebees are constant, but only butterflies can pollenate
all worlds.

Ignored, abandoned lilacs thrive, their insistent leaves trap scales
of dirt. To come to life is to embrace the dust zone. The crocus
succours wood ticks by orange prairie boulders, and beetles
on mown grass shiver in the wind. This marks the end of our
beginning, this air too dry. We drive on in a rattle of stones.

# In Flight

The man beside me
reads his Gospel Canticles
and Evening Prayers,
mutters Amen
with every lurch.

Two rows ahead
a baby shrieks.

The flight attendant offers
pretzels and rice crackers.
I keep the bag to read ingredients,
stop after thirty-four.

The woman in the seat in front
slumps back to sleep. I squirm
to find more leg room, twist
and smell sardines. Scent

rises from the floor.
The man behind me
from the Church
of No Deodorant
has just removed his shoes.

The plane won't land
for two more hours.

The sky is black.

Outside my window,

nothing

but one light

far off,

along the wingtip.

# The Visit

Gran holds out her wine glass
for the last inch of Spanish bubbly.
I refill the bowl of peanuts
she's eaten down to skins.

She's only here a week.
We offer privacy, respect.
Or is our care neglect,
a dread of aging?

At seventy, Gran canoed
alone on mirror lakes, skied
over frozen rivers.

At eighty-five, her greed is for
dregs of wine, the last peanut skins.

# Grasshopper Summer

A dry twig hangs on the patio gate,
mint in mocha shadows.

Highways have turned into oceans,
trucker tides rumble and ebb.

We're 5,000 miles from Utopia,
and phones channel tire treads,

dust from your wheels
rims the sky. It's a slow news day.

Anything can happen.
Dogs become mosquitoes

and distant barks whine high
upon the gate, a twig.

If everyone speaks, will anyone
answer? What will they say

about the silence?
The fire pit smolders.

I never told you that
he wrote; I kept his letters.

It's dark now. Will you call?
The gate twig flexes, flies.

# Watching Woman

Mary rises from the floor
of the old farmhouse.
The kitchen ceiling slices
hips, in upstairs bedrooms
pigeon droppings smear
her breasts.

On the roof, rusted strips
of tin and her head. Watching

woman stares
south to the fields.

No one is haying. No one
will come past the lilac windbreak
and the yellow caragana
to this empty farmhouse
and the dream
of dishes she once dried.

# Red

Even paper flowers wilt
in neglected rooms.
Dust on forgotten roses.

# Kiss of Knives

## 1: Mammogram

Foot on the pedal
        she drives the
plate

D
O
W
N

squeezes
my carved breast
to meet
each painted arch.

                One millimetre

                        two . . .

Longer
    flatter
    with each thrust.

Don't tense! she says.
Can't you hold still?

nerves

                ducts

                        muscles
flame

                                flesh.

DOWN

>The oven broiler
>sears my hand.

DOWN

>My bike skids
>I fly
>into grit and bloody knees.

DOWN

>The half-mad tabby
>sinks her teeth

deep

>into my thigh.

Raise your arm, now
turn, turn.

She pulls me
twists me

DIGS

>her fingers in my armpit

DRAGS

>soft tissue under Plexiglas

DRIVES it

D

O

W

N

## 2: Wings Spread Under Glass

The oncologist brings no pencil
to record his observations.
From the door of the exam room
he throws we-speak platitudes:

We're coping well with chemo

She's so tired, stomach churning
from scalp to fingernails, she can't walk
across a grocery store.

Studies don't show that.

Her husband travels.
She is alone.
Afraid.

Does anyone take notes
from participants with kids?

We're doing fine

Her son is one.
He's heard
her yell and cry more
than he's ever heard her
say that she loves him.

Her daughter's three.
Last night, she wrenched
her daughter's tiny arm and slapped her.

We're doing better than so many other patients

Measured by
 reports  images  samples
     blood                    breasts
bones.

### 3: Amber Absence

Orange
flows from plastic bladders
hooked above her head.

All colour is illusion,
wavelengths warped
by our perceptions.
Black absorbs all,
white reflects.

The liquid in those intravenous tubes:
everything but

orange

the only colour it rejects.

Oh, mix of methotrexate
and 5-fluorouracil

absorb every ray
but amber
        gold
colour of rain on autumn leaves
    tawny light of Prairie afternoons.

Orange energy deflect.

Her perception — in her mind.
Just like you hinted, doc?

You, who offered no solutions,
only tricks of MTX

and 5 FU.

## 4: Night Watch

Sometimes
when she can't sleep
she thinks of him
in darkness.

He had such power —
but less insight
than her Labrador Retriever.

No compassion,
          love.

Forgive?

She hopes
one day she will
at least forget
his blank stare.

But for today,
she hopes he's still alive,
barely, in some fourth-rate
nursing home

where he's grown
pudgy breasts
and earned the nickname

Nipples

for their firm
protrusion
through his backless
gown.

## 5: Close My Eyes

And go back twenty years.
Put my arms around that girl
Scared
  tired
    bewildered
exhausted
  scarred
          mad
If she sees what we will gain
(support
      respect
            love
from children
  husband
      self)
will she (ever) stop crying?

## 6: Again

That's an awful scar

Remind him
that he booked vacation
during your mastectomy.

What we really need is plastics

Remind him that
his resident, in thanks,
carved this puckered kiss.

I'll book you in

Tell him

again     again                again

 again!         AGAIN!

Not again.

They will never
touch your body
with their knives.

*7: Paper Patients*

have few side effects

work full-time
play golf and tennis
relish travel
romantic dinners
skiing with their kids
makeovers
and rave

about the inches they have
lost  and their high
blood counts

in journals and reports
they're not afraid

don't ask questions,
don't complain

they know the doctor's busy
know the doctor's right

## 8: *Scalpel Song*

down long green hallways
where patients wait in backless gowns

rubbing alcohol
swabbed cold across my hand

needles, toxins
in this house of knives

bury me in nausea
shuttered darkness

the doctor scans, samples, calibrates
clips, freezes, radiates

breasts          blood          bones
abandoning          abandonment

I am a specimen pinned to his pages
wings spread under glass

## 9: Hummingbirds

Ruby-throated
sip nectar
from deep bell flowers
as knives
kiss my chest.

Hummingbirds
hover, dip their beaks
in bougainvillea, crimson
petals cup their throats.

I dream I reclaim
my breasts'
absent flesh.

# Lemons and Leather

The plane takes off in darkness,
Snow crusted to the wings.
The sun won't rise for hours.
I'm soaring west by night.

Snow crusted to the wings,
Drawn on by dreams of heat.
I'm soaring west by night,
Eyes swollen with lost sleep.

Drawn on by dreams of heat,
And half-remembered stories.
Eyes swollen with lost sleep,
I watch a galaxy of farms,

And half-remember stories —
Queens in velvet gowns.
I watch a galaxy of farms,
Are children happy on the ground?

Queens in velvet gowns.
Royal blue, with diamonds.
Are children happy on the ground?
The windows fill with clouds,

Royal blue, with diamonds.
Pineapples fell first, then cloves.
The windows fill with clouds.
I called you Mommy then.

Pineapples fell first, then cloves.
I'm older now, too old to cry.
I called you Mommy then.
Lemons and leather are almost gone.

I'm older now, too old to cry.
Don't lose the smoke or strawberries.
Lemons and leather are almost gone.
I count the stars: Please don't forget me.

Don't lose the smoke or strawberries.
The plane takes off in darkness.
I count the stars — please don't forget me.
The sun won't rise for hours.

# March Flight

Late morning and the spice cupboard begins to throb.
I am alone. You're on the coast at meetings last night,
at a salmon barbecue with my retired preacher dad.
I see him in the pulpit still, black-robed and praying for grace.

Bottles domino. Saffron smashes garlic. Coriander crushes
thyme. A thump, a flutter. Doors thrust open. Fury
iridescent, a black bird streaks across the room, smacks
against a pane. A white greasy ghost on glass.

A wild bird. Grackle. Its purple fear. Out
across the kitchen, into the fireplace, onto the sofa. I open
all the doors and windows, but it dives at me, yellow eyes
and bill wide. And then a breeze, breath

of grass and lilacs. The grackle grasps its freedom,
veers over the patio, the neighbour's roof to the rising draught.
I scald the little bottles, scan the walls for cracks.

Late afternoon, they phone to say my father's heart has stopped.
He was walking to McDonald's for his coffee. It skipped
one beat, and then another. They tried hard to save him.
In the mall, the ambulance, Emergency, Intensive, Coronary
Care . . .

He fought hard to leave.

# January Ground

A metal marker
snowdrifted to your name

a lily, gelled brown
from the cold

the pinecone I carried
past the cedar hedge

placed above your heart,
your grave so new that

lumps of clay jut
through the snow —

I wonder why
they didn't rake it.

# Diagnosis

Last week

the cliché of all lovers
I said you'd live with me

forever.

Tonight, your
backbone
    snags my fingers.

gait      unbalances
  voice
        scratches air.

Squamous cell.

A mouthful, baby.
Not poetic.

But now we will learn
what your alley-cat dad
could never teach you.

The Big C.

# Window Ledge

Your fur is matted,
and I haven't seen you
eat for four long days.

The vet said
they could cut away
the cancer
and your jaw.

That won't cure.

Last night, you struggled
up onto my bed, curled
in beside me,
purred.

Now, you're perched
on the window ledge,
turned away from sparrows,
head bobbing in the sun.

# Nightshade

Not morning, when slow
release pain killers unfurl blue
lilies on your abscessed jaw, calm
your tremors, warm your paws.

Not noon, when you crouch
in the linen closet, bleed
on violet sheets, burrow deeper
when I say your name.

Not night, when you fumble
your cat circles, too stiff
to lie beside me. I fold your legs,
then hug you. *Purring.*

Not morning, noon, or night,
but a moment out of time
when I can't hear
your long, hoarse cry,
can't see your last shed hairs.

Won't feel again
your head, too full of poppies,
droop.

# Sunflowers

Beyond the graveyard
rows of hollow golden stalks.
Heads bowed and broken
no longer follow
the winter sun.

# Tattered Wings

On this April morning wind keens
the corner, rasps the window, shrieks,

and I mourn the child who heard
a song whenever branches creaked.

I am pitched to thunder clouds, a monarch
thrashed off course on tattered wings.

My nights are lightning, my days rain.
If I could, I would return to listen

to your sting, brace for breath to rush
through me, taste, devour, sing.

# Spring

Above the field
snow geese thread
waves in April's
cirrus.

Wingtips black
and bellies shining,
they eddy in an updraft.

*Whouk, whouk,* the chorus.
Praise for snow melt,
instant lakes, and
new grass, grain.

# The Mission Field

One day, her parents buy a dog
and Vancouver's mountain peaks burst high above her window
and she runs down bright streets with the small black streak
until her parents hear

the Call.

Quarantine is cruel.
They give away the dog.

New friends,
Aunties, mangos, avocados,
a mint-green house and a skinny puppy
with one thin, white stripe.

Then the next move
and the next, her parents
busy serving God.
She just wants another dog.

Selfish to want so much
when people are in
real
true
need.

She gives away her doll's lace dresses.

Molly's canvas limbs grow
mildew without clothes.

# Vacant Lot, Kingston, Jamaica

We wait until the man tumbles
from sleep, fumbles his spliff,
trails his cows back up the mountain,

then we root through dirt and rusted
tins for stones to pelt the tamarinds.

Suck sour-sweet pulp
from glossy seeds.

Indian date, gypsy tree,
sailing over a bitter sea,
an immigrant, like me,

a child
of tuques and tamaracks,
not curry, chutney, tangerines.

# Flat Island

Opal rain in a churning coral sea.
When I imagine thirty feet of water

Toppled palms, and beaches
that disappear and reappear,
sand dunes on the road

crashing across your shoreline
through your silent boarded towns

No gasoline or cooking fuel,
drinking water, schools,
or working phones

leaving a wake of salt, sand, rubble,
I see only pounding opal rain.

# Green Mangos

Tonight
I want to go

for curried goat
at midnight
        after dancing.

I want to eat
green mangos.

Swim in turquoise.

Breathe.

# Praise

For this hot bath
and for this book
damp pages curling

For the crackle
from the kitchen
pot roast braised

For garlic and
for oranges

# To the Woman

I saw standing at the stoplight
reading in the rain, scarlet
puddles at your feet,
hair slicked back.

You never looked up
at the signal or the cars,
tire splash, light flash,
so rapt within your story.

This is all there is.
Who desired who, and why.
Who endured what, and how.
Who ventured where,
and when.

Now.

This.

One moment.
Puddles, rain.

# If You Read This

Don't mistake me
for someone
who scatters
heat and winter
on these pages.

Who turns
wind-swayed birches
into disco balls
of hoar frost.

Who writes it down,
her cursor blinking,
thirty seconds from the birches,
thirty years from disco nights.

Don't pretend
to know her
if we meet.

When she reaches
the last line
she'll disappear.

# Notes on the Poems

"It's all about Pi" includes mathematical terms relating to Pi/ϖ (the never-ending, non-repeating 3.14159265358979323846264338 . . . to the first 26 decimal places).

"Lemons and Leather" touches on research that indicates a relationship between the inability to recognize certain scents and the development of Alzheimer's disease.

"Midnight" refers to a study by University of Texas researchers Meston and Buss, which identified 237 reasons why humans have sex.

"Swordfish" is a found poem, from text describing complex patterns in number puzzles from an online Sudoku Guide.

"Watching Woman" was inspired by Heather Benning's "Marysburg Project: Watching Woman", at Marysburg, Saskatchewan.